# AUTHOR NOTES

Cataloging-in-Publication Data has been applied for and may be obtained from the Library of Congress.

ISBN: 978-1-947215-17-7

How to Draw Cute Animals with Joseph Stevenson text and illustrations copyright 2020 Golden Valley Publishing, LLC. Coloring with Joseph Stevenson are trademarks of Golden Valley Publishing and the design of this book's jacket is a trade dress of Golden Valley Publishing. All rights reserved.

Book design by Joseph Stevenson Cover design by Joseph Stevenson

Printed and bound in U.S.A.

An imprint of Golden Valley Press, LLC
PO BOX 531412 Henderson, NV 89052
www.josephstevenson.com

# DRAWING A DOG

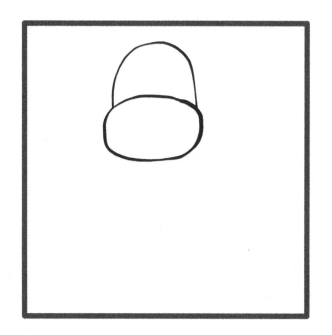

# PRACTICE

# DRAWING A TURTLE

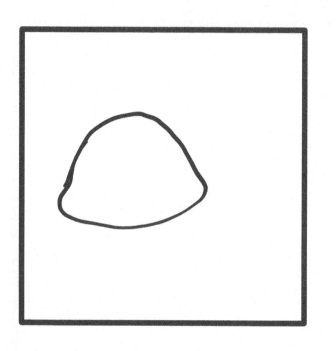

# PRACTICE

# DRAWING A DOLPHIN

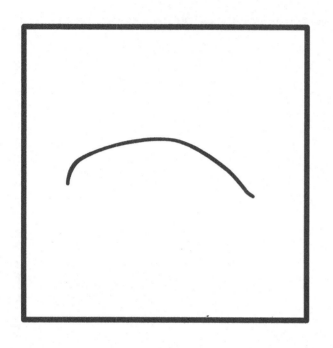

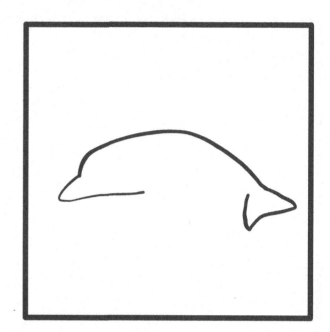

# PRACTICE

# DRAWING A FOX

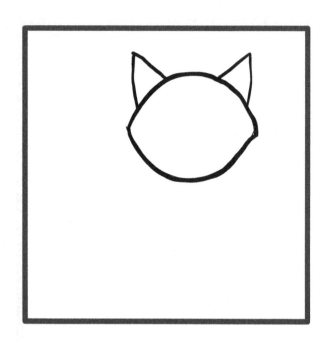

# PRACTICE

# DRAWING A LADYBUG

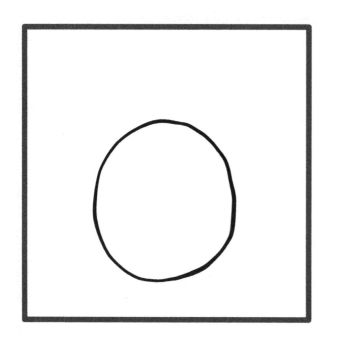

# PRACTICE

# DRAWING A BUTTERFLY

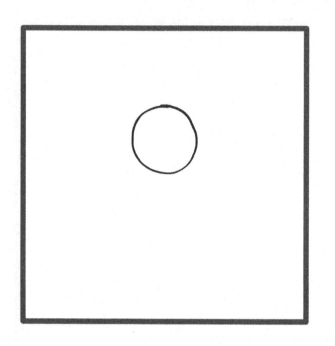

# PRACTICE

# DRAWING A SHARK

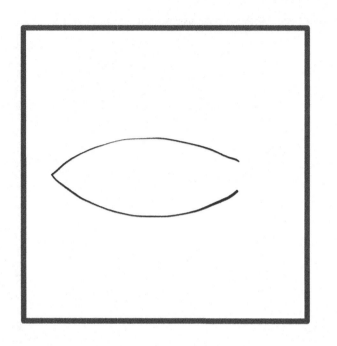
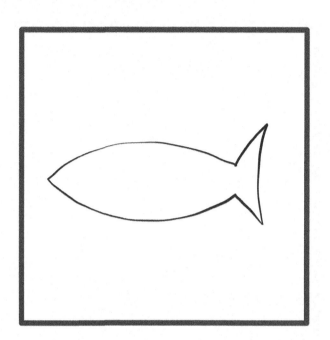

# PRACTICE

# DRAWING A BEE

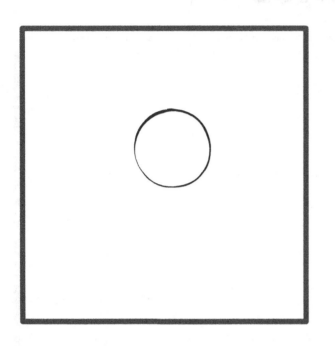
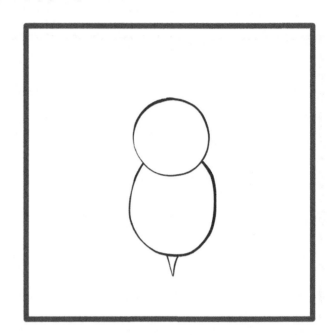

# PRACTICE

# DRAWING A SNAIL

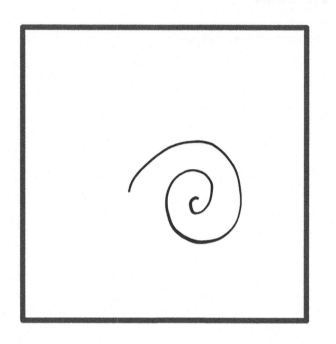

# PRACTICE

# DRAWING A SPIDER

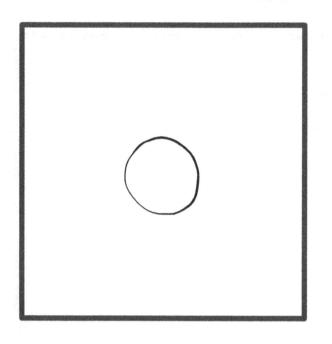

# PRACTICE

# DRAWING A WHALE

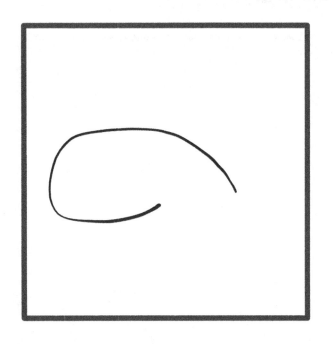

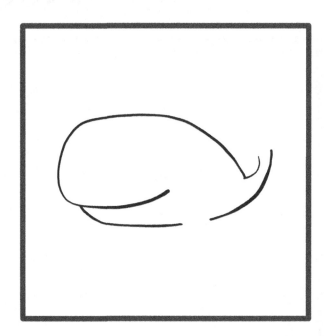

# PRACTICE

# DRAWING A OCTOPUS

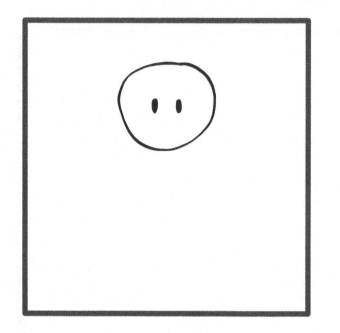

# PRACTICE

# DRAWING A COW

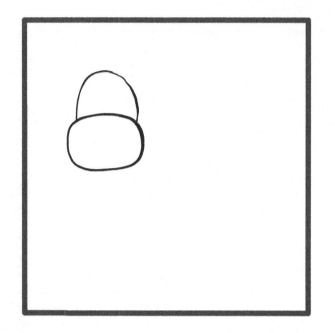

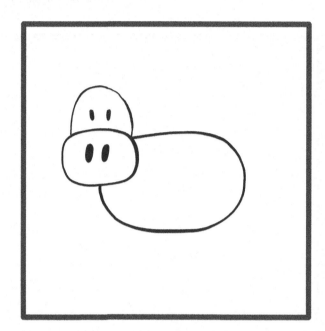

# PRACTICE

# DRAWING A CAT

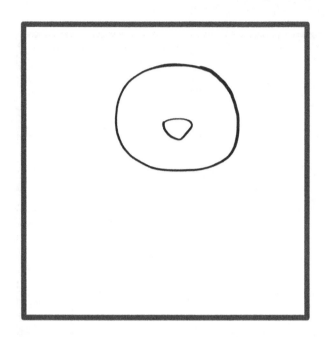

# PRACTICE

# DRAWING A OWL

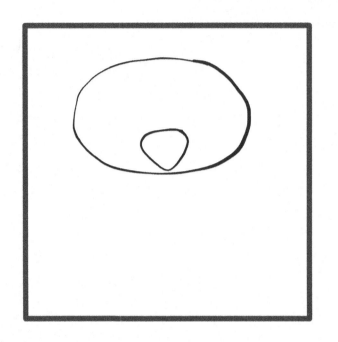

# PRACTICE

# DRAWING A DOG

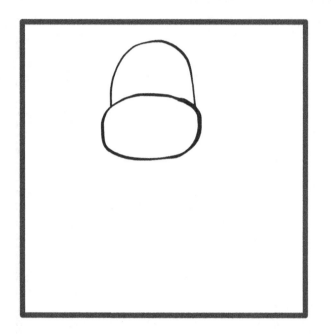

# PRACTICE

# DRAWING A HORSE

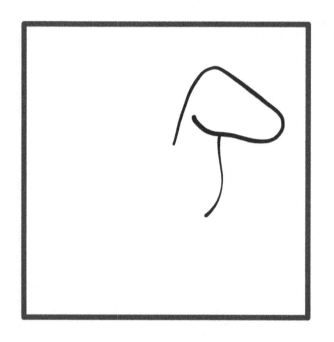

# PRACTICE

# DRAWING A SHEEP

# PRACTICE

# DRAWING A FROG

# PRACTICE

# DRAWING A GIRAFFE

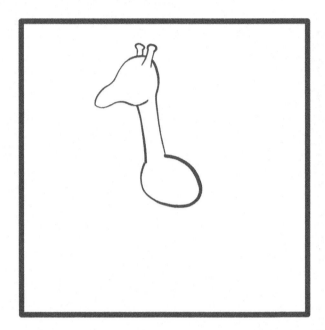

# PRACTICE

# DRAWING A ELEPHANT

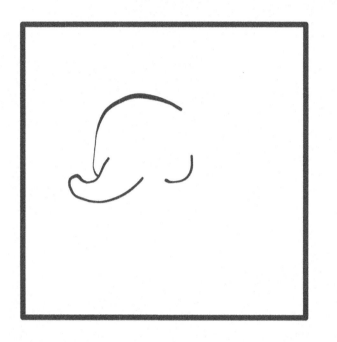

# PRACTICE

Made in the USA
Coppell, TX
10 December 2020